Messi: A Boy Who Became A Star.

Copyright © 2017 by Steve Herman

ISBN-13: 978-1974634118
ISBN-10: 1974634116

First Edition: August 2017
10 9 8 7 6 5 4 3 2 1

Messi was born in 1987, in Argentina,
a country that loved soccer,
which is known as football there.

His parents worked hard to provide for Messi and his three siblings. His mother worked in a magnet factory while his father managed a factory that produced steel.

To unwind after a long day of work, Messi's parents loved watching and playing soccer.
They taught Messi how to play, and by the time he was four, his dad was also his coach.

Even as a young child, Messi knew he wanted to grow up to be a soccer superstar, so he kept practicing. With the help of his family, his small legs grew strong.

By six, he was on his own soccer team. Despite being young, he treated the game like he was playing in the big leagues, and scored about 500 goals by the time he was in middle school.

Messi faced many obstacles on his way
to becoming a player.
At 10, the age when most kids were
growing a lot, he was not.
His growth had come to a stop because
of a medical condition that prevented
him from growing.

He may have been small, but his determination was large.
While his father helped him get the medicine he needed to keep growing, he proved to his teammates that sometimes size doesn't matter.

As he grew, he continued to prove his worth. He soon joined Barcelona, one of the biggest soccer clubs in Spain.

Other obstacles kept getting in his way.
He once broke his cheekbone, and had to wear a protector.
He found it annoying, and took a risk by taking it off.

And he won the game!
Even when he was injured, his willpower led his team to victory.

He never grew as tall as the other children, but with his shorter size, he was quick and could run very fast, plus his legs were strong enough to kick the ball into the goal.

At 30, he is now one of the biggest soccer players in the world, and he continues to get even better.
His motivation to be the best player possible, no matter what stands in his way, helped him achieve success.

Another thing that helped him was support. His parents saw soccer as more than just a silly pastime.
To them, soccer was a way of life, and they passed their love for it down to Messi and the whole family enjoyed it together.

Whatever you want to achieve as you grow up, surround yourself with people who will encourage you and push you toward your goals.

Messi couldn't have won the game without a team, and neither can you. So get out there and find the team that is right for you and keep working toward your goal.

No matter what obstacles may come your way, learn from Messi and treat it like a soccer ball and kick it away.

Just like Messi, you too can be a star. You just need hard work, teammates, and a love for what you do.

Thank you for reading my story!
Did you like the book?
If you like it, please write a review on Amazon.
Tell me what you think!
I look forward to reading your review!

Read the story of Ronaldo!

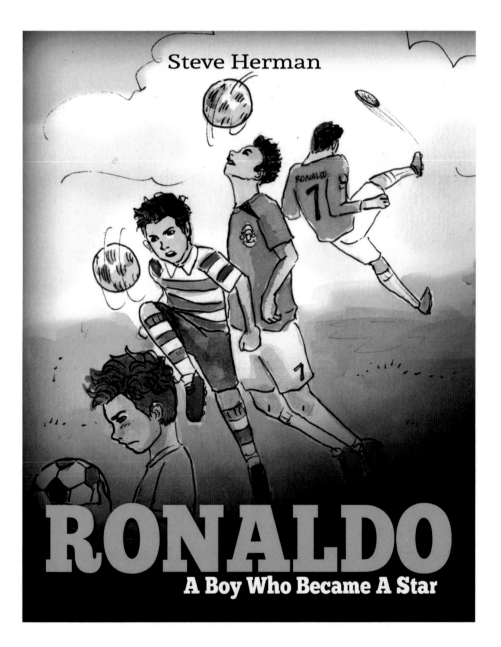

Steve Herman

RONALDO
A Boy Who Became A Star

Made in the USA
Middletown, DE
13 December 2022

18499295R00024